Copyright © 2023 by Shalom Greenwald
All rights reserved. No part of this book, whole or in part, may be stored, reproduced, transmitted or translated in any form or by any means whatsoever, manually or electronically, without prior written permission from the copyright holder, except by a reviewer who wishes to quote brief passages in connection with a review written for inclusion in newspapers or magazines. The rights of the copyright holder will be strictly enforced.

Credits:
Editing by Ian Grinblat of Crafted Expression
Weis Printing Pty Ltd, Melbourne, Australia
ADVENTURE BOOKS, Melbourne 2023

ISBN 9780645585711

ADVENTUREBOOKS.COM.AU

A a

A - Alpha
.−

Always accept others

B b

B - Bravo
— • • •

Be nice to your sisters and to your **b**rothers

C c

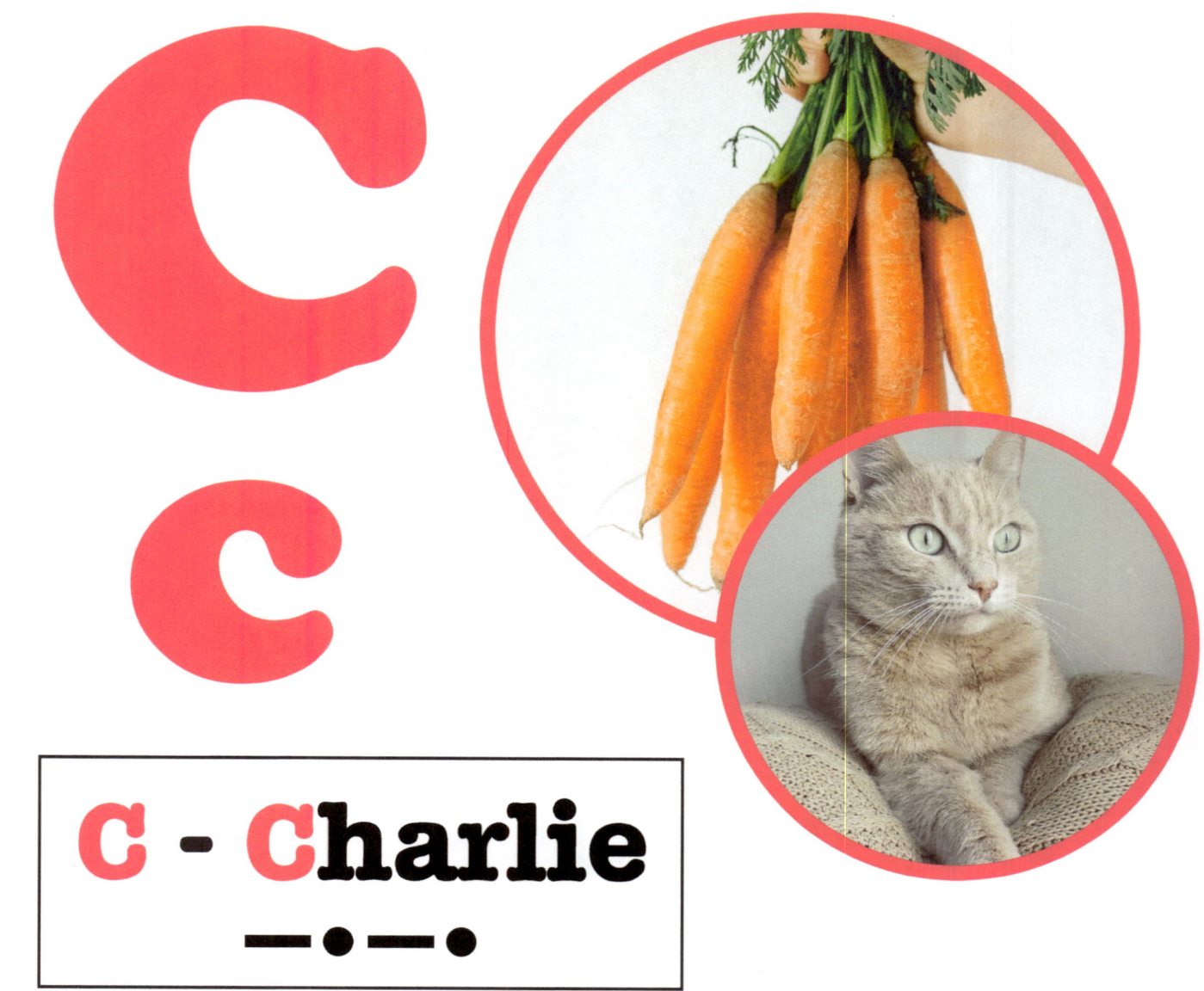

C - Charlie
— • — •

Clean up when you're done

3

Dd

D - Delta
—··

Dance an**d** have fun

4

E e

E - Echo

Enjoy life every day

F f

F - **F**oxtrot

· · — ·

Friends, come over and play!

G g

G - **G**olf
--.

Grateful to hear and to see

H h

H - Hotel
....

Happy, so **h**appy, to be fabulous me!

I i

I - India

I love to share

J j

J - **J**uliett
·———

Justice means fair

10

K k

K - Kilo

—·—

Kindness to animals from big to small

11

L l

L - Lima
• — • •

Listen to everyone, yes, one and all

M m

M - Mike

Mum and Dad are the best

N n

N - **N**overnber
— •

Naptime, perfect time to rest!

O o

O - Oscar
___

Of c**o**urse, manners are imp**o**rtant t**oo**

P p

P - Papa

Please, excuse me and thank you!

Q q

Q - Quebec
— — · —

Question: Can I please help you out?

R r

R - **R**omeo
•—•

Respectful tone! Please don't shout!

S s

S - Sierra
...

Safety first, I'm sure you know

T t

T - Tango

Teamwork's best wherever you go.

U u

U - Uniform
•• —

Understand health, always eat right

21

V v

v - Victor
···−

Veggies and fruit are best, so don't put up a fight

W w

W - **W**hiskey
• — —

Wash your hands, always be neat

23

X x

x - **x**ray

—··—

e**x**cited to splash puddles with your feet

Y y

Y - Yankee
— • — —

Yes, you can do it! So sing or say:

Z z

z - **z**ulu
− − · ·

zip a dee doo dah, what a fabulous day!

MORSE CODE

Samuel Morse was one of the inventors of the electrical telegraph, a long-distance communication system using electrical pulses and the silence between them. It was used from the 1840s until the late 20th Century.

Each electrical pulse was generated by a hand-operated key and was received as a sound.

Morse Telegraph Transmitter

Samuel Morse was one of the inventors of the electrical telegraph, a long-distance communication system using electrical pulses and the silence between them. It was used from the 1840s until the late 20th Century.

Each electrical pulse was generated by a hand-operated key and was received as a sound.

Morse Telegraph Register which emitted a sound when activated by an electrical pulse

Before the invention of telephone or radio communication, the telegraph was extremely important. During the American Civil War, a telegraph station was installed in President Abraham Lincoln's bedroom and the telegraph operator slept in the room, ready to receive important news.

Morse and his collaborator, Alfred Vail, designed the code so that the most frequently used letters in the alphabet have the least number of dots and dashes. For example, the letter E is one single dot.

Morse code can be sent between ships using powerful flashlights.

The international distress signal, SOS, is three dots followed by three dashes, and then three dots again.

MORSE CODE

Letter	Code		Letter	Code
A	·−		U	··−
B	−···		V	···−
C	−·−·		W	·−−
D	−··		X	−··−
E	·		Y	−·−−
F	··−·		Z	−−··
G	−−·			
H	····			
I	··			
J	·−−−			
K	−·−		1	·−−−−
L	·−··		2	··−−−
M	−−		3	···−−
N	−·		4	····−
O	−−−		5	·····
P	·−−·		6	−····
Q	−−·−		7	−−···
R	·−·		8	−−−··
S	···		9	−−−−·
T	−		10	−−−−−

29

The NATO Phonetic Alphabet

The NATO Phonetic Alphabet is a spelling alphabet used to ensure that letters are clearly understood even when speech is distorted or hard to hear when communicating over radio or telephone.

It was developed in the 1950s and is used by airline pilots, police, members of the military, and other officials. Here are the letters in the NATO phonetic alphabet:

- **A**lfa (or Alpha)
- **B**ravo
- **C**harlie
- **D**elta
- **E**cho
- **F**oxtrot
- **G**olf
- **H**otel
- **I**ndia
- **J**uliet (or Juliett)
- **K**ilo
- **L**ima
- **M**ike
- **N**ovember
- **O**scar
- **P**apa
- **Q**uebec
- **R**omeo
- **S**ierra
- **T**ango
- **U**niform
- **V**ictor
- **W**hiskey
- **X**-ray
- **Y**ankee
- **Z**ulu

How the NATO Phonetic Alphabet Is Used

The NATO phonetic alphabet is always used to enhance safety. Air traffic controllers, for example, use the NATO Phonetic Alphabet to communicate with pilots, and this is especially important when they would otherwise be difficult to understand. If they wanted to identify plane KLM, they would call it, "Kilo Lima Mike." If they wanted to tell a pilot to land on strip F, they would say, "Land on Foxtrot."

Morse Code

A	•—	J	•———	S	•••
B	—•••	K	—•—	T	—
C	—•—•	L	•—••	U	••—
D	—••	M	——	V	•••—
E	•	N	—•	W	•——
F	••—•	O	———	X	—••—
G	——•	P	•——•	Y	—•——
H	••••	Q	——•—	Z	——••
I	••	R	•—•		

Can you write your name?

Can you solve these two riddles?

1. Aim high and reach for the stars.

2. Keep up the good work.

As an exercise, try writing – or typing - a sentence in Morse code. It is easier than you might think, but there are some basic rules.

As you can see from the Morse code chart, only two letters are represented by just one signal · E which is a single dot, and T which is a single dash. All of the other letters of the alphabet are represented by a combination of between two and five signals, so by keeping to these rules you will keep your message clear.

If you haven't memorised the Morse code alphabet, you will need a wall chart or a printed sheet as your reference to know the combinations of the characters in your message.

There are two ways to write - or type – a Morse code message:

The simpler way is to write the actual dot and dash signals themselves.
The word "hello" appears as " •••• • •—•• •—•• ——— "

1.The second option is to spell the dot and dash signal using "dit" for a dot and "dah" for a dash. Using this method, the word "hello" appears as "di-di-di-dit dit di-dah-di-dit di-dah-di-dit dah-dah-dah"

As you can see, this method requires 56 keystrokes, including spaces, compared with only 20 keystrokes in example a, above.

2. The second basic rule is to leave a space after each letter in a word; if you don't, you will mix your signals and make it almost impossible to read.

3. To make the meaning clear, put a slash after completing the spelling of a word. It also helps if you leave a space on each side of each slash.

Using slashes, "I Love You" written in Morse code is,

" •• / •—•• ——— •••— • / —•—— ——— ••— "

4. There are no capital letters in Morse code because they would add unwanted complexity to the code.

The spacing is key to understanding Morse code messages no matter if it is tapped, written, or even spoken. If the duration of a dot is taken to be one unit, then the duration of a dash is three units, the space between the components of one character is one unit, the space between characters is three units and between words seven units.

www.ingramcontent.com/pod-product-compliance
Lightning Source LLC
Chambersburg PA
CBHW041200290426
44109CB00002B/78